Two African Countries

Elizabeth Paren and Gill Stacey

PACIFIC
L E A R N I N G

© 2004 **Pacific Learning**
© 2001 Written by **Elizabeth Paren** and **Gill Stacey**
Illustrated by **Petra Röhr-Rouéndaal**
Photography: Ashanti Gold: p. 23 (top); Botswanacraft: p. 26 (both); Corel: pp. 6 (left), 25 (top), (middle), 27 (bottom right); De Beers: p. 19 (left); Hutchison Library/Michael Macintyre: p. 16 (right); Hutchison Library/M. Kahn: p. 22 (top); Hutchison Library/Mary Jelliffe: p. 22 (middle); Hutchison Library/Crispin Hughes: p. 30; Hutchison Library/Liba Taylor: p. 23 (bottom); Illustrative Options: p. 9 (bottom); Images of Africa Photobank/David Keith Jones: p. 7 (left); Images of Africa/Vanessa Burger: p. 7 (bottom right), 27; Images of Africa Photobank/Carla Signorini Jones: p. 9 (top); Panos Pictures/Trygve Bolstad: p. 10 (left); Panos Pictures/Liba Taylor: p. 11 (middle); Panos Pictures/David Reed: pp. 14 (top), 17 (bottom), 22 (bottom); Panos Pictures/Caroline Penn: p. 17 (top); Panos Pictures/Betty Press: p. 20 (left); Panos Pictures/Bruce Paton: p. 21 (left); Panos Pictures/Steve Thomas: p. 29 (top); Robert Estall Photo Library/Carol Beckwith/Angela Fisher: pp. 24 (top), (bottom), 25 (bottom,); Petra Röhr-Rouéndaal: pp. 5 (left), 11 (left), 12, 21 (top); Still Pictures/Ron Giling: p. 4 (top right); Still Pictures/E. Duigenan – Christian Aid: p. 4 (bottom left); Still Pictures/Jorgen Schytte: pp. (right), 10 (right), 13 (top right), 15 (top), 16 (left), 20 (right), 28 (bottom); Still Pictures/Jonas Ekstromer: p. 18 (left); Still Pictures/Chris Caldicott: p. 28 (top); Tropix/M. Auckland: pp. 5 (right), (bottom), 29 (bottom); Tropix/M.-V. Birley: p. 8; Tropix/J Woollard: pp. 13 (middle), 19 (right); Tropix/Brydon: p. 14 (bottom); Tropix/G. Roberts: p. 18 (bottom).
Front cover: Petra Röhr-Rouéndaal (top right); Botswanacraft (bottom left); Corel (background)
Back cover: Robert Estall Photo Library/Carol Beckwith/Angela Fisher
Maps on pp. 6–8 are by **Richard Morris**
Globes by **Geo Atlas**
U.S. edit by **Rebecca McEwen**

This Americanized Edition of *Two African Countries*, originally published in England in 2001, is published by arrangement with Oxford University Press.

08 07 06 05 04
10 9 8 7 6 5 4 3 2 1

Published by
Pacific Learning
P.O. Box 2723
Huntington Beach, CA 92647-0723
www.pacificlearning.com

ISBN: 1-59055-412-4
PL-7423

Printed in China.

Contents

Welcome to Botswana and Ghana

There are forty-seven countries in Africa. In this book we will look at two of them, Botswana and Ghana.

Botswana and Ghana have a lot in common. For example, they are both young countries, with a high proportion of the population under the age of eighteen.

This book looks at other similarities between the two countries – and at many differences too.

FACT BOX		Botswana	Ghana
	Population	about 1.5 million	about 18 million
	Capital	Gaborone	Accra
	Main peoples	Setswana, Kalanga	Akan, Ewe, Mole-Dagomba

The flag of Botswana

Blue for water: water is very precious to the people of Botswana.

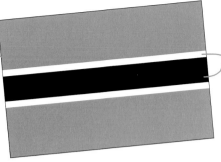

White and black for the people: these colors show how the people live peacefully together.

The flag of Ghana

Red for the blood of freedom fighters

Gold for the minerals

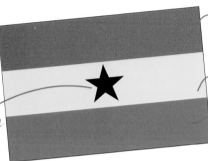

The black star for African freedom

Green for the land

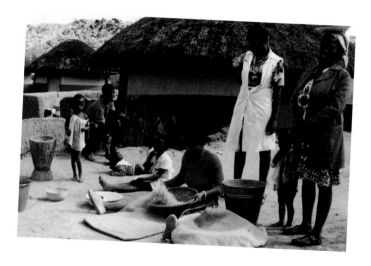

This book is about the everyday lives of people in these two African countries. It tells you what the children learn at school, what they do when they go home, and where they go shopping. It might also make you want to visit Ghana and Botswana one day!

What Is the Land Like?

Ghana is a country in west Africa. It lies in the **tropics**, just north of the equator in the Tropic of Cancer.

Most of the land in Ghana is flat and less than 500 feet (150 m) above sea level.

The coast of Ghana is more than 310 miles (500 km) long. Behind it are saltwater **lagoons** and low-lying **plains**.

Tropic of Cancer

Lake Volta, in the center of Ghana, is the world's largest human-made lake. It is 250 miles (400 km) long. The dams at Akosombo and Kpong provide most of Ghana's electricity.

About one-third of Ghana is rain forest. In the north, there are fewer trees and more grassland.

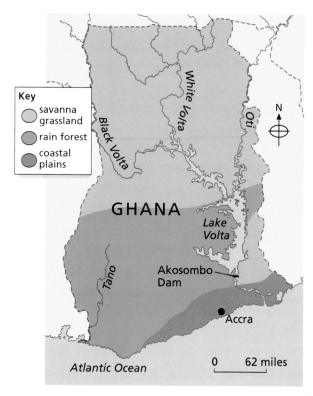

Key
- savanna grassland
- rain forest
- coastal plains

White Volta

Black Volta

Oti

N

GHANA

Lake Volta

Tano

Akosombo Dam

Accra

Atlantic Ocean

0   62 miles

Two thousand, five hundred miles (4,023 km) away from Ghana is Botswana. It lies south of the equator, and the Tropic of Capricorn crosses the country. Botswana has no coastline.

— Tropic of Capricorn

Most of Botswana is about 3,600 feet (1,100 m) above sea level and forms a basin that is part of the Kalahari, which is mostly semidesert with dry grassland and short trees.

In the southwest the land is desert, where little grows.

▲
In northwest Botswana, the Okavango River spreads out in a wide **delta**. The water sinks into the sand, leaving a huge **swamp**.

A game reserve in the central Kalahari

▼

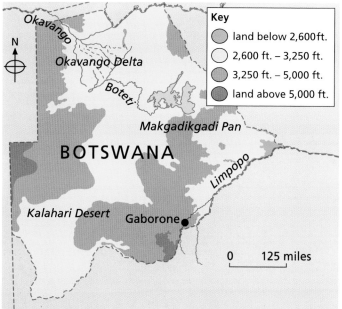

Key
○ land below 2,600 ft.
○ 2,600 ft. – 3,250 ft.
○ 3,250 ft. – 5,000 ft.
○ land above 5,000 ft.

N

Okavango
Okavango Delta
Boteti
Makgadikgadi Pan
BOTSWANA
Limpopo
Kalahari Desert   Gaborone●

0   125 miles

What Is the Weather Like?

Both Ghana and Botswana lie in the tropics. However, their climates are very different.

Ghana has a tropical climate. There are two main seasons: the dry season and the rainy season. It is hot almost all year long. In the day, the temperature often reaches 86°F (30°C).

The dry season lasts from November to March. The weather is hot and dry in the north. In the south it is hot and very humid.

In the dry season, the **harmattan** wind blows in from the Sahara Desert. It brings cooler nights and covers everything with fine dust and sand.

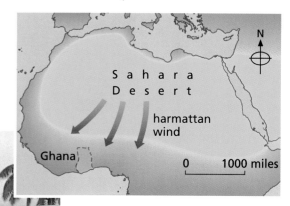

These graphs show the rainfall in the two capital cities.

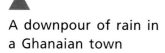

A downpour of rain in a Ghanaian town

The rainy season lasts from April to October. There are thunderstorms and very heavy rainfall. In between the storms, the days are hot and sunny.

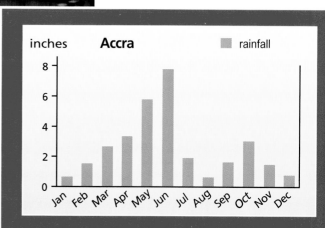

The seasons in Botswana are more like those in Europe, with a definite difference between summer and winter.

Summer lasts from November to April. This is when it rains, with thunderstorms in the late afternoon. Often there is not enough rain, and the farmers worry about their crops.

▲

Summer days in Botswana are hot, with temperatures sometimes reaching 86°F (30°C).

Batswana dress up warmly for the winter days. ▶

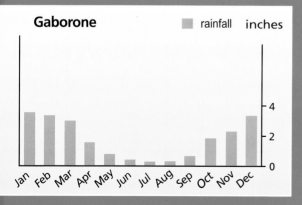

Winter lasts from May to October. Then the days can be warm but dry, and the nights can be cold. Sometimes there are frosts.

Going to Primary School

In both countries, most children walk to school.
Some of them have to walk several miles.

 A primary classroom in Botswana

An outside classroom in Ghana

Some primary schools have bright classrooms with chairs, tables, and plenty of materials. However, many schools have basic furniture and few materials.

FACT BOX		
Ghana	**Botswana**	
School starts at 8:30 a.m. and finishes at 3:30 p.m.	School starts at 7 a.m. and finishes at 12:30 p.m.	
Children learn in their own language.	Children learn in their own language until Year 3, which is similar to third grade in the United States. Then they learn in English.	
Most children learn math, science, religion, English, history, and life skills.	Children learn Setswana, math, English, science, and social studies.	
Children have to wear school uniforms. Most wear the same colors – yellow and brown.	Most children wear school uniforms.	

Kwabena is from Ghana.
He is saying:
My name is Kwabena. What's your name?
Kwabena's own language is Twi.

Ye fre me Kwabena. Ye frewo sen?

Neo is from Botswana.
She is saying:
My name is Neo. What's your name?
Neo's own language is Setswana.

Leina lame ke Neo. Leina la gago ke mang?

Free Time

During free time or recess, all children like to have a snack. They may bring their own food, or they may buy from women who sell food outside the school.

In both countries, children like to eat fruit. In Ghana, fried **plantain**, roasted **maize**, peanuts, and doughballs are popular snacks. Some Batswana children bring potato chips and sandwiches. Many have bread and tea.

This Ghanaian woman is cooking and selling doughballs.

At free time, children play games. Boys prefer soccer. Girls often play skipping or jumping games.

These Batswana children are playing a dancing game on the playground.

11

After School

All children have chores to do when they return from school. This girl, like many others, does chores around the home.

Walking home from school

Looking after little brother

Drinking tea

Cleaning

Fetching water from the well

Helping prepare food

Doing homework

Playing

Children may work to help earn money for the family.

◄ These Ghanaian girls are selling tomatoes in the market.

Boys have to do their homework too. In Ghana they might then help with the fishing or work on the cocoa farm. Some boys take care of cattle.

Boys in Botswana have to care for cattle or goats. They might collect firewood in a donkey cart.

This Ghanaian boy is helping fishermen with their nets. His payment will be a bucket of fish.

These Batswana boys are taking a break from their herding.

Some children, mostly in the towns, are lucky enough to have televisions or computers.

Children in towns still have to do some chores. They might go to the store, take care of younger brothers or sisters, prepare food, or help in the garden.

They play the same kinds of games as children in the **rural** areas. Soccer is always popular.

13

Farming and Food

In both countries many people live in rural areas. Every family farms some land. Some men and women are full-time farmers; some also work other jobs.

Most farmers grow food for their own families. Families usually have only a small plot of land and do most of the work by hand. Most families keep animals, such as chickens or goats.

A Batswana woman weeds the maize crop. Women do most of the daily work on the farm. ▶

Here are just some of the food crops that are grown in Ghana.

YAM

OKRA MANGO MAIZE ONIONS PLANTAIN

GHANA

Ghanaians like spicy food. They eat a **starch** dish with meat or vegetable stew. The most popular starch dish is *fufu*, which is made from yams or **cassava**.

In Ghana, many small farmers also grow some crops to sell. The most important crop is cocoa.

Women work hard to pound the *fufu* until it is completely smooth. ▶

These Ghanaian women are threshing. People in both countries always help each other when there is extra work to be done on the farm, such as clearing the land or bringing in the harvest.

Here are just some of the food crops that are grown in Botswana.

Some Batswana like to eat mopane worms. These are the **larvae** of the mopane moth. People collect the worms from mopane trees, then dry the worms and store them.

MELON

MILLET

BEANS

SPINACH

MAIZE

BOTSWANA

The dried mopane worms are first steamed and then fried. They are full of protein and minerals.

Many Batswana families own cows. The cows provide beef to sell and also show how wealthy a family is.

Family Life in Rural Areas

Many members of a family often live together. There may be grandparents, married sons and their wives, and all their children. This is called an extended family.

In rural areas in Ghana, each extended family lives in a compound. The compound is made up of several buildings for different members of the family.

Family compounds in a village near Accra ▶

◀ Ghanaian women do all the cooking. They may have an indoor kitchen or an outdoor cooking area.

Women and men have their own separate areas for sleeping, cooking, and eating. Young children eat and sleep with their mothers.

- Children in both countries are seen as a blessing to the family.
- All the adults help raise the children.
- Children are expected to always show respect to their elders.
- Children may go live with other relatives for a few years.

In Botswana, many families have always lived in very large villages. The chief and his family live in the middle of the village. There is a special enclosure for the chief's cattle. The rest of the village is divided into sections called wards. Groups of related families live in each ward. Each also has its own cattle enclosure.

Batswana villages are spread over a very wide area. Some villages have as many as 40,000 people.

Today, these large villages also have good roads, shops, schools, and offices.

Living in the Towns and Cities

In both Ghana and Botswana, more and more people live in towns and cities. Some people are well-off and live in big houses. For most people, life is more difficult. They have to live in poorer, crowded areas.

What is daily life like in the capital cities, Accra and Gaborone?

Most people get to work by bus, minibus or shared taxi.

The streets of Accra are always crowded. Street vendors are everywhere, selling newspapers, roasted nuts, candy — even lottery tickets.

Accra is a lively, modern city with many business and government offices, stores, busy markets, museums, and apartment buildings.

eople may work in ctories, stores, or ffices.

Some people have their own small businesses.

People like to eat out. Fast food is also very popular.

There are many places to go after work.

Watching sports, especially soccer, is a popular weekend activity in Botswana. Large crowds fill the Gaborone sports stadium to watch a variety of events.

Many people work as diamond sorters in Gaborone. Diamonds from Botswana are used to make jewelry all over the world.

All Kinds of Shopping

Markets are the most popular place for shopping in Ghana. Ghanaians go to market both to buy and to sell. Markets are also the place to meet friends and catch up on the latest gossip.

In the larger markets people can buy almost anything. Many of the most successful traders in Ghana are women.

Department stores and supermarkets are popular places to shop in the towns, although prices are usually higher than in the markets.

People can also buy things from roadside stalls. Traders and farmers sell food such as pineapples, mangoes, and yams. People traveling out from the towns find these prices much lower.

Market prices are not fixed. Traders and customers always bargain before a price is settled.

In Batswana towns, people do their shopping in small shops, supermarkets, or in shopping malls.

Some traders sell goods by the side of the road. Some sell cheap watches or grass brooms, but many sell fruit and vegetables. There are also carpenters, who will make custom furniture.

The mall in Gaborone is where everyone likes to meet and shop.

Batswana who live in rural areas can buy everyday items at the village store. Many people drive into town once a month to buy all the other things they need.

Village stores sell things such as salt, sugar, soap, matches, clothes, pots, and pans.

A Changing World

New and better roads, fast-growing towns, and modern technology are changing Botswana and Ghana. Many people are leaving rural areas to work in factories, offices, and mines.

Botswana was once very poor. Today, it is one of the richest countries in Africa. Its wealth comes from diamonds and other minerals found in the desert.

Gaborone is one of the fastest growing cities in the world.

Changing Lives: The San People of the Desert

The San once moved around the desert, finding everything they needed. They collected underground water and stored it in ostrich eggshells. They gathered fruit and seeds, and hunted wild animals. They liked to tell stories around the fire.

This San woman is making beads from ostrich eggshells.

Today, mines, cattle farms, and game reserves are spreading into the desert. The San have had to find homes and work elsewhere.

These San people have had to leave their desert homes.

Ghana is not a rich country, but its people are working hard to improve their lives. They hope that the **export** of gold will help them do this.

Modern machinery is used to process Ghanaian gold.

Changing Lives: Women in Ghana

Many men now leave their village homes to work in the towns and cities. Women often have to raise children and take care of the farms on their own.

In the past, Ghanaians believed that education was more important for boys than girls. Today, many more girls go to school and find good jobs.

Cooperatives are organizations that help women work together to learn new skills and earn money for their families. These Ghanaian women work in a sewing cooperative.

Ghana – Land of Gold

The Power of Gold

There has always been gold in Ghana. More than 300 years ago, there was a forest kingdom called Ashanti. Its wealth and power came from gold.

The most important **symbol**, even today, of the power of the Ashanti people is the Golden Stool. This stool is solid gold. It is so precious that it is hidden away and is only seen on very special occasions.

The Golden Stool has the place of honor next to the Ashanti king at this celebration.

Kente Cloth

The most famous craft in Ghana is weaving Kente cloth. Kente comes in many different colors and patterns. Each design is given a special name.

Once, only kings and queens could wear Kente. Today, it is the national costume for all Ghanaians but is worn only for special occasions.

This girl is wearing Kente cloth and gold jewelry at a Ghanaian festival.

Festivals

There are festivals throughout Ghana every month of the year. Everyone enjoys festivals. They are a chance to dress up, to follow colorful processions, to listen to traditional music, and to dance.

Every festival has a special meaning. Festivals remind people of important events in the past. People show respect to their traditional leaders and honor their religious traditions.

Festivals are often celebrated with music and dance. ▶

Only men are allowed to weave Kente, and the craft has always been passed from father to son. Gilbert "Bobbo" Ahiagble is a master weaver. When he was three his father began to teach him about weaving.

In 1999, Bobbo opened a school where he teaches students to weave traditional Kente cloth.

Baskets and Storytelling in Botswana

Making Baskets

For hundreds of years, people in the north of Botswana have made baskets. They use them for storing food.

Today, many baskets are for sale. Their beautiful designs sell all over the world.

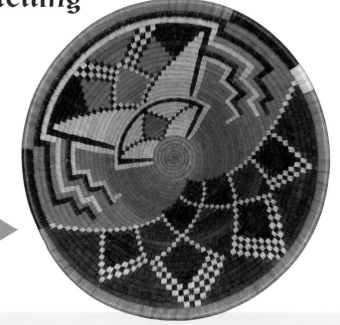

Mahurero Twapika

Mahurero lives with her family near the Okavango Delta. She is one of more than 2,000 women who make baskets. Mahurero's baskets have won prizes. Sometimes she visits Gaborone and teaches children how to make baskets.

Making baskets is hard work. Mahurero has to walk or ride on a donkey for half a day to find the palm shoots she needs. She cuts the shoots into strips and boils them with natural dyes. Then she can start weaving. It takes her a month to weave one basket.

Telling Stories

Batswana people love to tell stories. This story is told by the San people.

San people believe that a person's spirit can live in an animal's body.

Long ago, all the people and animals lived peacefully under the Earth with Kaang, the Lord of all Life. They always had light.

Kaang created a world above the Earth. First, he made an enormous tree. Then he dug a hole. He led the people and the animals through the hole up to the foot of the tree. Kaang told the people not to build any fires.

When it got dark the people were cold and frightened. They lit a fire, but the fire frightened the animals away. The people and animals would not live together anymore.

Vacations with a Difference

It is only recently that tourists have discovered the attractions of Ghana and Botswana.

Ghana – Land of Smiles

Enjoy Ghana's Coast
Laze on the beautiful palm-fringed beaches. Windsurf in the Atlantic Ocean. Explore the unspoiled fishing villages.

Discover Our Rich Past
Visit the ancient coastal forts and castles. Travel inland to Kumasi – heart of the great Ashanti Kingdom. Head north to the ancient mosque of Larabanga.

Explore Ghana's Natural Beauty
See the rain forest from up high – along the treetop canopy walkway of Kakum National Park. See elephants and lions in Mole National Park. Take a boat ride on Lake Volta.

Bask in the Warmth of Ghana
Bargain for crafts in the colorful markets. Share the excitement of our festivals.

Our country is the friendliest in west Africa!

Visit Botswana – For the Vacation of a Lifetime!

Visit the Okavango Delta

Step into your *mekoro* – the canoe that will take you through a tranquil world of lilies and grasses. Watch the hippos, see the fish, hear the haunting cry of the fish eagle. Watch a sunset you will never forget.

Visit Chobe National Park

At dawn, see Chobe's mighty elephants come out of the forest to drink. Watch thousands of zebra migrate across the wide open plains.

Visit the Tsodilo Hills

See amazing rock paintings in these remote hills. Find out how people and animals were living thousands of years ago.

Visit the Craft Markets

Choose a beautifully made souvenir of Botswana to take home. Will it be a basket, some jewelry, or a wall hanging? It will be hard to choose.

Conclusion

In Ghana and Botswana, people's everyday lives are quite similar.

- Most children live in rural areas and go to primary schools.
- Many are brought up in extended families.
- Most children have to do household chores before they play.
- People grow the food they eat and buy in the market what they cannot grow.
- Life in the towns is also similar, with people doing all kinds of work. Here, there are stores, offices, supermarkets, sports stadiums, movie theaters, and, usually, too many cars.
- Modern technology is beginning to change people's lives, especially in the towns. Office workers often use computers. Some people use the Internet. Cell phones are popular everywhere.

There are many differences as well.

The people in the two countries speak different languages and like different food. Their customs, the way they celebrate special occasions, and their music and dancing are different too.

Glossary

Batswana – the people of Botswana (can be used as a noun and as an adjective)

cassava – a kind of tropical plant that has starchy, edible roots

delta – low-lying land where a river divides into many small branches

export – to sell things to another country

harmattan – a dry wind that carries sand and dust. It blows south from the Sahara Desert, usually during December and January.

lagoon – a lake of sea water

larvae – the young of an insect, after they emerge from the egg and before they develop wings

maize – a type of grain, also known as corn. Maize can be cooked, used to make flour or oil, or to feed cattle

plain – a large area of flat land

plantain – yellow or green fruit from a tropical plant. Plantain looks like a large banana, but is cooked as a vegetable.

rural – relating to the countryside, where most people live in villages and farm the land

starch – food that may be eaten as the main part of a meal, such as potatoes, rice, or yams

swamp – an area of low land that is full of water

symbol – something that represents a person or an idea. For example, the Golden Stool is the symbol of the Ashanti people.

tropics – the area of the Earth's surface that lies between the Tropics of Capricorn and Cancer. These are imaginary lines of latitude drawn around the Earth.

Index